Y0-DJQ-588

For kids who know
that learning can be fun
and filled with song!

We acknowledge the financial support of
the Government of Canada through the Book
Publishing Industry Development Program
(BPIDP) for our publishing activities

Canadä

Lyrics by Blaine Selkirk

Music by Sara Jordan

Produced and Published by
℗ ©1992 Sara Jordan Publishing
a division of Jordan Music Productions Inc.
(SOCAN)

1st edition, ©1992
2nd edition, ©1994
3rd edition, ©2001

ISBN: 1-894262-48-4

Acknowledgments

Producer, Composer - Sara Jordan
Lyricist - Blaine Selkirk
Consulting Editor - Sara Stratton
Male Singer and Rapper - Blaine Selkirk
Female Singers - Gail Selkirk, Shantall Young
Recording Engineer, Special Effects - Mark Shannon
Digital Illustration Assistant - Ishrat Rahim, Darryl Taylor
Recording Engineer - Mark Shannon, Toronto
Cover Design and Layout - Campbell Creative Services
                          - Neglia Design
Digitally Recorded and Mixed by Mark Shannon,
Toronto, Ontario, 1992, 1994 and 2001.

This lyrics-activity book may be reproduced by the classroom teacher for whom it was purchased, but may not be copied for an entire school or school district.

Drawings of the Presidents:
From The New Book of Knowledge, 1989 Edition.
Copyright © 1989 by Grolier Incorporated. Reprinted with permission.

For further information contact:

Jordan Music Productions Inc.
M.P.O. Box 490
Niagara Falls, NY
U.S.A. 14302-0490

Jordan Music Productions Inc.
Station M, Box 160
Toronto, Ontario
Canada, M6S 4T3

Internet: http://www.sara-jordan.com
E-mail: sjordan@sara-jordan.com
Telephone: 1-800-567-7733

℗ © 1992, 1994, 2001 Sara Jordan and
Jordan Music Productions Inc. (SOCAN)
All rights reserved.

Table of Contents

Hints for Teachers

and Parents

As both a teacher and parent dealing with young people every day, I know how hard it is sometimes to interest them in reading or studying about history.

The intent of *The Presidents' Rap*® is to bring to life the history of the American Presidents, from Washington to George W. Bush, through the rhythm and melodies of over a dozen upbeat tunes written within the musical style of each historical period.

History need not be something that is studied during a certain block of time each day, but something that is carried over into many areas of study, from vocal music class to gym, from drama to creative writing.

Most educators agree that the literacy problem we face, is not so much one of illiteracy, but aliteracy (choosing not to read). In a fast-paced society where we are bombarded with television, videos, music, and arcade games, *The Presidents' Rap*® kit approaches both history and reading in a new, up-beat, and fun way.

Sincerely

Sara Jordan

President

A few ways to use *The Presidents' Rap*® Kit:

In the classroom:

☑ *The Presidents' Rap*® can be used as an introduction or wrap-up to the study of the various periods of American History. Students tend to memorize factual information easily, when it is presented in the rhyme of a song.

☑ *The Presidents' Rap*® works well in independent learning centers with headphones and as a remedial tutor for students.

☑ As part of a drama class, have the students act out the various songs. Great fun for "air-band" shows.

☑ Encourage students to visit the library, and write their own lyrics about favorite Presidents as part of a creative writing assignment.

At home:

At home, whether you listen on the family stereo, through a stereo headset, or in the car as you run errands, *The Presidents' Rap*® is great fun and entertainment for the entire family.

☑ Try quizzing each other on historical facts found in the songs. You'll find that young readers will take an avid interest in reading through the lyrics book in search of the answers!

☑ Try singing along using the lyrics book. Maybe you'll discover a star in your own home, or at the very least a budding history buff!

What is a President?

chorus:

What is a President? What does he do?
What does he try to do for me and you?
He's only human and he does the best he can,
Looking out for every woman, child and man.

Imagine you and a friend can't get along.
You think you're right and your friend is wrong.
But even though you may not like the debate,
It's freedom of speech that makes
    our country great.

And that freedom comes from the Constitution.
That was signed after the American Revolution.
This document straightened out a lot of things,
And it gave us a man to look after those things.

chorus:

What is a President? What does he do?
What does he try to do for me and you?
He's only human and he does the best he can
Looking out for every woman, child and man.

 The Presidents' Rap® ©1992, 1994, 2001 Sara Jordan Publishing

You see, the President leads us in war or peace.
He heads the Armed Forces as
    Commander-in-Chief.
He has to make decisions and take a stand
On the many different problems that face
    our land.

He lives in the White House in Washington,
But he's too busy working to have much fun.
If the people like what he does while he's there
He'll be re-elected for four more years.

chorus:

What is a President? What does he do?
What does he try to do for me and you?
He's only human and he does the best he can
Looking out for every woman, child and man.
Looking out for every woman, child and man.

George Washington

1789-1797

We take so much for granted in America today.
There've been so many changes; things weren't
always this way.
In 1789, you see, our country was so small,
Only four million people, just thirteen states in all.

We had a Constitution, but no one really knew
Just how the government would work or who
would see it through.
The man who was chosen to be President first
Came from Virginia, the place of his birth.

verse 1:

It is said that **George Washington** cut down a
cherry tree
And when he was caught he said, "I cannot tell a
lie."
It was this kind of honesty and courage that stayed
with him
To help guide America until the day he died.

During George Washington's time as President,
Congress passed the Bill of Rights.
He made many treaties with foreign nations,
So we could live in peace and not have to fight.

bridge:

He fought against the French when they
    threatened the colonies.
He tried his best to protect his home.
He once surrendered to superior forces
But he did his duty the best way known.

chorus:

All these things helped Washington be
    President.
He tried to do his best since his life began.
We all should follow Washington's example.
Always try to do the best that you can.

verse 2:

In 1759, he married Martha Custis
And settled down to life on his farm so fine.
In 1774, he was a delegate
When the Continental Congress met for the first
    time.

Chosen in '75 as General and
    Commander-in-Chief
Of the army that would battle for our freedoms
    and rights
The people were hoping for a quick victory
But he knew that it would be a very long fight.

bridge:

The Army spent a cold and dreary winter
Deep in the forest of Valley Forge.
But Washington was brave and never got
*   discouraged.*
He did his duty the best way known.

verse 3:

Finally the British were forced to surrender
At Yorktown in 1781.
Washington returned to his home in Virginia,
All the while thinking that his work was done

In 1787 he went to Philadelphia
To work on the Constitution there,
Creating a form of Federal government
That every person would find equal and fair.

bridge:

In 1789, he was elected President
The banner of freedom was finally flown
He served for two terms, leading America
He did his duty the best way known.

chorus:

All these things helped Washington be President.
He tried to do his best since his life began.
We all should follow Washington's example:
Always try to do the best that you can.

     The Presidents' Rap® ©1992, 1994, 2001 Sara Jordan Publishing

Adams, Jefferson, Madison & Monroe

chorus:

Adams, Jefferson, Madison, Monroe:
Under these men our country
would grow.
Things didn't always go exactly
as planned,
But a spirit of accomplishment
swept the land.

verse 1:

John Adams was the first Vice-
President.
He served under Washington, who
could forget?
He nominated Washington to lead in our defense
And introduced the Stars and Stripes with
reverence.

John Adams
1797-1801

Adams became President in 1797.
It seemed to the country he was sent from heaven.
He tried to avert war with France.
He only wanted peace, leaving nothing to chance.

chorus:

verse 2:

Here's a good question that makes a
lot of sense.
Who wrote the Declaration of
Independence?
His name was
Thomas Jefferson, a
writer and inventor.
A scientist, musician, and
political mentor.

As the third President, Jefferson
was wise.
The Louisiana Purchase made us
double in size.
He retired to his home in Virginia nearby,
And died in 1826, the 4th of July.

Thomas
Jefferson
1801-1809

chorus:

verse 3:

James Madison was the Father
of the Constitution.
He did the very best he could
to offer a solution
That would be acceptable to a
majority of States
During the final Constitutional
debates.

James Madison   1809-1817

      The Presidents' Rap® ©1992, 1994, 2001 Sara Jordan Publishing

The War of 1812 was fought against the British,
And many brave men would die before the finish,
But in the end the war was won
At the Battle of New Orleans under General
    Jackson.

chorus:

verse 4:

James Monroe ushered in the
    "Era of Good Feelings".
America was prosperous,
    strong for many reasons.
He annexed Florida; the
    country grew
But there's one more thing that's
    important for you.

In 1823 he declared the Monroe
    Doctrine,
Which said that no European nations
    could walk in
And invade any countries in our hemisphere.
If they did, he said the United States would
    interfere.

James Munroe
1817-1825

chorus:

Oh! What a Time It Was

chorus:

These were times so exciting that I bet
These were times that nobody can forget
Our Presidents tried but couldn't do more
As they tried to prevent a civil war.

verse 1:

John Quincy Adams
   became the President;
Oh! What a time it was...
In 1825 to the White House
   he went.
Oh! What a time it was...
His father was John Adams who
   we've seen before.
Oh! What a time it was...
Father and son, they both knew the score.
Oh! What a time it was...

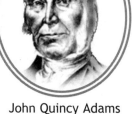

John Quincy Adams
1825-1829

Adams had a tough time getting things done
'Cause the Congress wouldn't pass his legislation.
After he was President he didn't disappear;
He served as a Congressman for seventeen years.

chorus:

verse 2:

Andrew Jackson settled in
the state of Tennessee.
Oh! What a time it was...
When he was just a boy he
showed his bravery.
Oh! What a time it was...
He joined the Army, a General
he became.
Oh! What a time it was...
In the Battle of New Orleans he
won much fame.
Oh! What a time it was...

Andrew Jackson
1829-1837

"Old Hickory" was President in 1829;
He made South Carolina tow the line.
In 1835 he paid off the national debt.
Every sort of challenge Andrew Jackson met.

chorus:

verse 3:

Martin Van Buren served in a
lot of roles,
Oh! What a time it was...
But to be our 8th President
was his goal.
Oh! What a time it was...

Martin Van Buren
1837-1841

In 1837 a Depression came
Oh! What a time it was...
And Martin Van Buren was held to blame.
Oh! What a time it was...

William Harrison won the
    Battle of Tippecanoe,
His campaign slogan,
    "Tippecanoe and Tyler, too."
But in 1841 after 30 days
Our ninth President died, the
    first to leave that way.

William Henry Harrison
1841

chorus:

verse 4:

John Tyler was the Vice-President
Oh! What a time it was.
Who became President after
    Harrison's death.
Oh! What a time it was...
A Governor, a Senator, a
    Congressman:
Oh! What a time it was...
All these things John Tyler had
    done.!
Oh! What a time it was...

John Tyler
1841-1845

     The Presidents' Rap®   ©1992, 1994, 2001 Sara Jordan Publishing

He signed a treaty with China that started trade.
Under Tyler more states were made.
Florida became the twenty-seventh one
And Texas soon followed as the West was won.

chorus:

James Polk did what he thought
    was right.
Oh! What a time it was...
His slogan was "54-40 or Fight".
Oh! What a time it was...
To get the Oregon Territory
    was his goal,
Oh! What a time it was...
And to win California from
    Mexico.
Oh! What a time it was...

James Polk
1845-1849

'Cause a whole lot of settlers
    were heading west
And they needed land, all that we possessed.
After war with Mexico it all came to be;
America finally stretched from sea to sea.

chorus:

Our 12th President was
Zachary Taylor.
Oh! What a time it was...
"Old Rough and Ready" was
   one tough soldier.
Oh! What a time it was...
A hero of the war with Mexico,
Oh! What a time it was...
He did his best to keep the
   country whole.
Oh! What a time it was...

Zachary Taylor
1849-1850

When new states were created, his plan seemed
   wise;
He tried to get the North and South to compromise
But he died in office after only 2 years
The nation mourned; there were many tears.

chorus:

verse 6

After Taylor died **Millard
   Fillmore** became
Oh! What a time it was...
The 13th President with
   problems the same
Oh! What a time it was...

Millard Fillmore
1850-1853

He opened up Japan to Western trade,
Oh! What a time it was...
And our nation stayed together for
    another decade.
Oh! What a time it was...

Franklin Pierce was the 14th man
To be the President of our growing
    land.
He won more territory in the West.
And to prevent Civil War he did his best.

Franklin Pierce
1853-1857

chorus:

In 1857 a new President came
Oh! What a time it was...
And **James Buchanan** was his name.
Oh! What a time it was...
He tried to stop the war between
    the states,
Oh! What a time it was...
But between the North and South
    there was too much hate.
Oh! What a time it was..

James Buchanan
1857-1861

By the start of 1861,
Seven slave states had left the Union.
Buchanan tried his best to unite the land,
But America's only Civil War began.

chorus: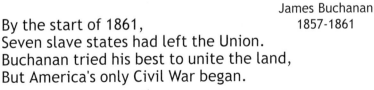

The Spirit of Lincoln

1861-1865

chorus 2x:

*The spirit of **Abraham Lincoln***
Lives in us today
The love he had for his fellow man
Showed America the way.

verse 1:

Our 16th President came from the West
From the state of Illinois.
In a small log cabin he was born
That's all he knew as a boy.

On the frontier there weren't many schools.
He walked so many miles
Just to borrow books so he could learn
And prepare him for his future trials.

chorus 2x:

verse 2:

He went on a trip to New Orleans
Back in 1831.
It was there that he saw the misery
That slavery had begun.

He studied hard for many years;
A lawyer he became.
He did his legal work so well,
He was known as "Honest Abe".

chorus 2x:

verse 3:

"A house divided against itself
Cannot stand."
Abe Lincoln ran for President
As he tried to unite the land.

But war broke out between the states
In 1861.
Both sides fought for four long years
With many battles lost and won.

bridge:

Because of Lincoln's vision
Of a nation strong and free,
He proclaimed an end to slavery
Back in 1863.

chorus 2x:

verse 4:

He gave a famous speech one day
That stood above the rest.
Those words still live in our memory
As the Gettysburg Address.

By 1865 the war was won,
But Lincoln never lived to see
The country reunited
In peace and harmony.

bridge:

He was killed by a single bullet
From John Wilkes Booth's gun.
The nation mourned, both North and South,
For a great man's life was done.

chorus 2x:

    The Presidents' Rap® ©1992, 1994, 2001 Sara Jordan Publishing

Stronger Than Before

(Johnson, Grant, Hayes & Garfield)

chorus:

The country needed healing
After so much war destruction.
This ushered in the Era of
*   Reconstruction.*
Looking to the future
Was the President's chore,
To put it back together
Stronger than before.

verse 1:

After Lincoln was assassinated,
    nobody knew,
How **Andrew Johnson** as
    President would do.
He had to lead the nation
    after years of war.
He had nothing to guide him.
    No one had before.

Andrew Johnson
1865-1869

Johnson treated the South like Lincoln would.
He didn't want to punish them, like others
    if they could.
His honesty and stubbornness led to a fight,
But Johnson was convinced that he was right.

bridge:

In his second term he was almost impeached.
A stalemate with Congress had been reached.
They wanted to take away Presidential power,
But Johnson was acquitted and saved the hour.

chorus:

verse 2:

Ulysses S. Grant became our
    President
'Cause we needed someone
    who was competent.
Grant had led the Northern
    armies in the Civil War;
His military genius you couldn't
    ignore.

Ulysses S. Grant
1869-1877

 The Presidents' Rap® ©1992, 1994, 2001 Sara Jordan Publishing

The first transcontinental railway line
Ran to the Pacific during Grant's time.
He served two terms, passing the test.
Ulysses S. Grant always did his best.

chorus:

verse 3:

Rutherford Hayes was from Ohio.
The 19th man elected to go
To live in the White House in
    Washington.
A time of excitement for
    everyone.

He barely got elected since
    the vote was a tie.
It was up to the Congress to
    decide
Which man should be
    President and show no fear
In guiding the nation through these difficult
    years.

Rutherford B. Hayes
1877-1881

bridge:

He removed the last troops stationed in the South.
The people were relieved when they finally
    moved out,

'Cause it meant that our nation was finally whole.
Rutherford Hayes had achieved that goal.

chorus:

verse 4:

In 1880 **James Garfield** was
    elected.
Great accomplishments from
    him the people expected.
He had risen to the top from lowly
    birth.
In everything he did, he showed
    his worth.

James A. Garfield
1881

Garfield didn't get the chance to show what he
    could do.
An assassin's bullet meant that he was through.
He fought a brave fight and for a time survived,
But after 10 weeks he finally died.

chorus:

 The Presidents' Rap® ©1992, 1994, 2001 Sara Jordan Publishing

The Promised Land

(Arthur, Cleveland, Harrison, McKinley)

chorus:

The promised land, the promised land,
Millions came to the promised land,
So they could share the American Dream
In the promised land, the promised land.

verse 1:

Chester Arthur wanted to be
    President
In 1881 it wasn't his turn yet.
But when Garfield was killed,
His job Arthur filled.
Our Vice-President became
    the President.

Chester Arthur
1881-1885

Settlers headed west to help
    the country grow
And Arthur split the nation into equal time zones.
With the help of Congress, he reformed the
    civil service
'Cause Chester Arthur wanted it so.

chorus:

verse 2:

Grover Cleveland came in 1885,
Honest and hardworking, on the job he thrived.
If Congress passed a law that Cleveland thought was flawed,
He overrode it with a Presidential veto.

He stood for re-election in 1888;
It was very close but to lose was his fate.
But in 1892, he ran again, you see,
And won by a huge landslide victory.

Grover Cleveland
1885-89 & 1893-97

chorus:

verse 3:

Our next President was **Benjamin Harrison**,
A Civil War hero who was William Harrison's grandson.
He knew that our country was growing so fast:
Six new states created in a land so vast.

Benjamin Harrison
1889-1893

 The Presidents' Rap® ©1992, 1994, 2001 Sara Jordan Publishing

Harrison installed new electric lights
In the White House, where the atmosphere was
    always bright.
Prosperity! Prosperity!
When Harrison was President.

verse 4:

Now we're up to President
    number 25,
A man much admired while he
    was alive.
William McKinley was his
    name;
In 1897 to the White House he
    came.

William McKinley
1897-1901

We fought a war with Spain in 1898;
In Cuba and the Philippines the battle raged.
But when all was said and done, America won.
McKinley was the man who saved the day.

At Buffalo, New York in 1901
McKinley was killed by an assassin's gun.
Like Lincoln and Garfield who came before,
The nation was shocked and everyone mourned.

chorus:

The New Century
(Roosevelt, Taft, Wilson, Harding, Coolidge and Hoover)

verse 1:

Theodore Roosevelt had a thrill
When he led the Rough Riders up San Juan Hill.
His favorite saying if you had to pick, was
"Speak softly and carry a big stick."

And when McKinley died,
Theodore Roosevelt really tried
To do his best, to be first rate,
As the 26th President of the
    United States.

bridge:

*The Panama Canal he started
    to build
He won the Nobel Peace Prize,
    what a thrill.
His principles he wouldn't compromise;
Teddy cut the large corporations down to size.*

Theodore Roosevelt
1901-1909

Teddy was re-elected in 1904;
Everybody loved him even more.
Such a colorful President, and so active.
To America, Teddy had so much to give.

verse 2:

The next President was **William Taft**
Who had served the country doing many tasks.
Here at home and in the Philippines
He was no stranger to responsibility.

William Howard Taft
1909-1913

Taft created Arizona and New Mexico;
We were up to 48 states, you know.
He served one term - that was too short
Then became the Chief Justice of the Supreme Court.

bridge:

Woodrow Wilson wanted peace for everyone.
He tried to keep us out of World War One.
But war was declared in 1917,
And America fought against Germany

Woodrow Wilson
1913-1921

In 1918 came victory.
Wilson had a great idea, you see,
To found a League of Nations; that was wise.
For that he won the Nobel Prize.

Rap:

We got Prohibition, we got income tax,
Women got the right to vote that up 'til then they
    lacked.
Wilson was a man who worked so hard.
The nation held him with such
    high regard.

verse 3:

Warren Harding came to be
A victim of great tragedy.
In his government a scandal grew,
And nobody really knew what to do.

Warren G. Harding
1921-1923

'Cause Harding had become quite ill,
His Presidency went unfulfilled.
He died in 1923
And **Calvin Coolidge** made
    history.

bridge:

This was America's time in the
    sun.
The "Roaring Twenties" had
    begun.

Calvin Coolidge
1923-1929

How long it would last was any
    body's guess.
"The business of America is business."

The Presidents' Rap® ©1992, 1994, 2001 Sara Jordan Publishing

Those were the words that Coolidge spoke,
And the feeling was shared by every folk.
We were at peace and so content
When Calvin Coolidge was President.

Rap:

"A chicken in every pot,
A car in every garage"
Herbert Hoover wanted,
But it was a mirage.

'Cause in 1929,
The stock market crashed,
Left many unemployed
And without any cash.

Herbert Hoover
1929-1933

verse 4:

Hoover did everything he humanly could,
To stop the worst Depression we'd ever withstood.
By 1932, it was easy to see
That so many people lived in misery.

The Only Thing We Have to Fear (Roosevelt)

verse 1:

Franklin Delano Roosevelt
Was just like family most folks felt.
'Cause he was the President for so
    long
He sure deserves his own song.

He served for over 12 long
    years,
A time of triumph, a time of
    tears,
When he came to power in '33,
Roosevelt was ready to lead.

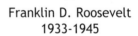

Franklin D. Roosevelt
1933-1945

bridge:

The Depression had everybody running scared.
Money was tight, but nobody dared
To make a move to fix the situation.
It was up to Roosevelt to rally the nation.

He made things happen in a faster way,
Dealing with problems every day,
Trying to motivate and co-ordinate,
Reviving the economy.

chorus:

"The only thing we have to fear is fear itself."
Roosevelt said this because he felt
A sense of empowerment's a sense of wealth.
"The only thing you have to fear is fear itself."

verse 2:

He got re-elected in '36.
There were still lots of things he had to fix.
Make work projects across the land,
For example, the Hoover Dam.

And social programs we now got
To improve ordinary people's lot.
Unemployment Insurance and Social Security
Gave us all dignity.

bridge:

He talked to the people that
Tuned in to his 'fireside chats'.
He was honest when saying how things should go,
As millions listened to him on the radio.

Earlier on, at the worst time,
Roosevelt'd had polio at age 39.
Because he'd faced this thing head-on
Roosevelt had grown very strong.

chorus:

verse 3:

The world could see the coming war.
Roosevelt kept the nation neutral once more.
But he helped some countries, our Allies,
Providing precious food and industrial supplies.

But finally in 1941,
Japan attacked Pearl Harbor;
    something had to be done.
We had to enter World War II
Against Japan, Germany and Italy too.

bridge:

But by the year 1945,
The Allies really turned the tide.
But Roosevelt didn't long survive;
It's a tragedy that he died.

He left a lasting legacy just for us,
His New Deal programs, his social justice.
For his contributions, his care and his fuss,
Franklin Roosevelt rates 'A plus'.

   The Presidents' Rap®   ©1992, 1994, 2001 Sara Jordan Publishing

This Cold War Stuff
(Truman, Eisenhower, Kennedy, Johnson, Nixon, Ford & Carter)

chorus:

Washington and Moscow in a deadly game;
Escalating tensions, both sides the same.
Building bigger weapons; calling their bluff.
Would the world survive all this Cold War stuff?

verse 1:

The Russians were our Allies during World War II.
By the end, decisions had to be made soon:
How to divide Europe into different
    spheres -
This division would cause so
    many tears.

Harry S. Truman came to be
Our 33rd President as we will
    see.
After Roosevelt had
    "Nothing left to fear."
Harry S. Truman said,
    "The buck stops here."

Harry S. Truman
1945-1953

When Truman had to stop Japan from doing more
He decided to use nuclear war.
So many were killed but lives were saved
Because Japan, America didn't have to invade.

chorus:

verse 2:

After the war we were rolling again.
The only thing that threatened was Communism.
The Soviets vowed to see it spread
Until Capitalism was very dead.

Truman was tough, he drew the line.
In 1950 it was time
To save Korea from the Communist threat.
After 3 bloody years the war would end.

chorus:

verse 3:

The President elected in 1952
Led the Allied forces during World War II
His name was **Dwight D. Eisenhower**;
He was always there when things went sour.

He had some success in foreign affairs,
Trying to save the world from nuclear nightmares.
He built Interstate Highways to get anywhere fast.
Peace and prosperity came together at last.

The Soviets launched a satellite called "Sputnik", you see,
We then launched "Explorer" and everyone agreed
That the race for space had started; it would never end
Eisenhower was strong; he would never bend.

Dwight D. Eisenhower
1953-1961

chorus:

verse 4:

John Fitzgerald Kennedy was 43
When in 1961 he got the Presidency.
The "New Frontier" was the vision he saw,
A blueprint to be followed by America.

He helped start the "Peace Corps" to work overseas
And helped to stamp out our country's racist disease.

John F. Kennedy
1961-1963

He also said that we should "shoot for the moon",
'Cause the scientific reward would be a boon.

The Soviet Union tried to put some missiles in
    Cuba, you see.
Brought our planet to the edge of World War III.
Kennedy was stubborn, he didn't back down,
Made the Soviets dismantle them and turn around.

Kennedy was killed by a sniper's gun.
After so much promise his life was done.
To remember his achievements and the life he
    gave,
An eternal flame burns to mark his grave.

chorus:

verse 5:

Lyndon Johnson knew the ins
    and outs
From a lifetime of government
    service jobs
A Congressman, Senator,
Vice-President too.
When Kennedy was killed he
    became President, too.

Lyndon B. Johnson
1963-1969

The Presidents' Rap® ©1992, 1994, 2001 Sara Jordan Publishing

Johnson had a vision of a "Great Society"
Where everyone was equal, strong and free.
He declared a war on poverty,
And brought in new health programs for the elderly.

Johnson was a champion of civil rights;
Against a lot of people he waged the fight.
He believed that everybody should have the same
Chance to be successful and to make a name.

He tried to fight the Communists in Viet Nam.
The war was getting bigger, but he took a stand
To beat them back and let freedom in;
But America was in a place they couldn't win.

chorus:

verse 6:

Richard Nixon was
Eisenhower's
    Vice-President,
In 1960 he ran for President.
But he lost the election to
    Kennedy.
For eight more years he wasn't
seen.

Richard Nixon
1969-1974

In 1968 he won the vote.
It was very close, we should note.
The first thing he did was try to win the peace
And sit down at the table with the North
    Vietnamese.

This giant step for mankind came
In 1969; this brought the astronauts fame.
But the protests against the war in Viet Nam
Demanded stronger action to bring peace to that
    land.

To do that he had to end the Cold War,
So he tried diplomacy with our Communist foes.
He went to China, and Russia too,
To make the world a safer place for me and you.

Nixon was the first President to resign.
In 1974, it took up all his time.
Answering to the scandal of Watergate,
He had to leave the White House in disgrace.

chorus:

     The Presidents' Rap®   ©1992, 1994, 2001 Sara Jordan Publishing

verse 7:

Gerald R. Ford was the Vice-
President
Who got the top job after
Nixon went.
He had been a Congressman
for 25 years.
He had much experience that
was clear.

Gerald R. Ford
1974-1977

He was the first President not to
be elected
'Cause as Vice-President he'd been appointed.
He continued on the path that Nixon had begun
In trying to make the world a safer one.

chorus:

verse 8:

Jimmy Carter came from a
small southern town.
He was a Naval officer who'd
been around.
A business man, a peanut
farmer from Georgia
he came.
In 1977 the Presidency
he claimed.

Jimmy Carter, Jr.
1977-1981

He moved to change the way the
    government works.
If it doesn't work efficiently, it drives us all berserk.
He got us to conserve during the energy crisis.
Expanded National Parks, the nation enjoyed this.

He engineered the Camp David Accord,
Between Israel and Egypt a deal was forged.
It brought about a friendship between ancient
    enemies,
Jimmy Carter should be proud because he did
    succeed.

Some Americans were held hostage in Iran.
Carter made every effort to free them.
He didn't succeed in making a deal,
And his bid for re-election failed.

chorus:

Washington and Moscow in a deadly game
Escalating tensions, both sides the same.
Building bigger weapons; calling their bluff.
Would the world survive all this Cold War stuff?

 The Presidents' Rap®   ©1992, 1994, 2001 Sara Jordan Publishing

The Wall Came Down

(Reagan and Bush)

chorus 2x

The Wall came down. The Wall came down.
The Iron Curtain parted and fell right down.
The world is safe for you and me
'Cause the Wall came down. The Wall came down.

Ronald Reagan makes for
   interesting lore.
Our 40th President was an actor
   before.
Getting into politics in
   California
This handsome movie idol led
   America.

To get out of recession he had a plan; Ronald W.
"Reaganomics" swept across the land. Reagan
To control the federal budget a solution 1981-1989
   was found,
And it turned economics upside down.

Someone tried to kill him in 1981,
But he was only wounded and recovered soon.
He was the oldest President in our history
But in dealing with our problems he had energy.

chorus 2x:

The people in Russia wanted a voice.
The Communist leadership had no choice
But to bring about democratic reform;
Gorbachev and Glasnost became the norm.

Reagan held out the olive branch
To help the Russians change, give them a fighting
    chance
Our nations formed a friendship that lasts to this
    day.
The shining sun melted the Cold War away.

chorus 2x:

George Bush held many jobs
    before.
A pilot in the Navy during the
    Second World War,
Ambassador to the United
    Nations,
A diplomat who served at the
    Chinese station,

A Congressman who had a lot
    to say,
And the Director of the CIA.
He served as Reagan's Vice-
    President;
In 1981 to the White House he went.

George H. W. Bush.
1989-1993

     The Presidents' Rap®   ©1992, 1994, 2001 Sara Jordan Publishing

During his term Communism collapsed.
The USSR's time was past
The Cold War was over, we were friends again.
The world was safe for women, children and men.

chorus 2x:

When Iraq invaded the country of Kuwait,
To right this injustice Bush couldn't wait.
He got the United Nations to join the cause,
And sent a strong army — he didn't pause.

The operation called "Desert Storm"
Liberated Kuwait, true to form.
George Bush showed the world that to be free
Is the way to peace and harmony.

chorus 2x:

The Wall came down. The Wall came down.
The Iron Curtain parted and fell right down.
The world is safe for you and me
'Cause the Wall came down. The Wall came down.

Time For a Change

(Bill Clinton)

verse 1:

George Bush had made a huge mark on the world.
Everywhere flags of peace were being unfurled.
But the Democrats knew that the people were
    tired.
They chose a candidate who was truly inspired.

bridge:

Bill Clinton *campaigned like a*
    man possessed.
When the votes were counted
    he was ahead of the rest.
He was a Rhodes Scholar who
    then studied law
and soon became the Governor
    of Arkansas.

Bill Clinton
1993-2001

chorus:

    The Presidents' Rap® ©1992, 1994, 2001 Sara Jordan Publishing

It was time for a change.
It was time for a change.
He came from the south, down in Arkansas.
It was time for a change.
It was time for a change.

verse 2:

He tried to reform Health Care,
    to make it more fair.
But the Republican Congress blocked his efforts
    there.
He sent our troops to Bosnia and Kosovo too
Stopping Serbia's 'ethnic cleansing', he had to do.

bridge:

He oversaw the longest economic boom
As Americans watched the stock market zoom.
He worked hard to mediate a Middle Eastern
    peace,
And balanced the Federal budget, saw inflation
    decrease.

verse 3:

After being re-elected in '96
A scandal erupted, something he couldn't fix
He escaped impeachment at his Senate trial
How he's judged by history, we'll have to wait
    awhile.

chorus:

The Journey Had Begun

(George W. Bush)

verse 1

The Millenium election was
  a bitter battle.
The outcome was in doubt.
To win a majority in the
  Electoral College,
Depended on a state in the
  south.

George W. Bush
2001-

The vote count in Florida,
Was the subject of dispute.
Recounts stopped, a winner declared,
After taking the Supreme Court route.

*Though **George W. Bush** lost the popular vote,*
He was the candidate who had won.
He was a President's son.
He was a President's son.

Raised in the state of Texas,
He was a man who got things done.
The journey had begun.
The journey had begun.

 The Presidents' Rap® ©1992, 1994, 2001 Sara Jordan Publishing

verse 2:

His family was famous. His father led the nation
As our fortieth President,
And the spirit of leadership and public service,
From the father to son it went.

He had been successful
in the oilfields of his state
and owned the Texas Rangers baseball team,
but politics couldn't wait.

He served two terms as governor
Showing that he had
The skill to lead us all.
The skill to lead us all.

Strong family values, tax cuts,
And a higher education standard
Was his campaign call.
Was his campaign call.

He was a President's son
The journey had begun.

He was a President's son
The journey had begun.

He was a President's son
The journey had begun.

Ask your retailer about other excellent audio programs by teacher, Sara Jordan

Bilingual Songs™ Volumes 1-4

*** Parents' Choice Award Winner! ***

The perfect way to have fun while acquiring a second language. This series teaches the basic alphabet, counting to 100, days of the week, months of the year, greetings, colors, food, animals, parts of the body, clothing, family members, emotions, places in the community and the countryside, measurement, opposites, gender, articles, plural forms of nouns, adjectives, pronouns, adverbs of frequency, question words and much more! ENGLISH-SPANISH and ENGLISH-FRENCH

Funky Phonics®: Learn to Read, Volumes 1-4

Blending the best in educational research and practice, Sara Jordan's four part series provides students with the strategies needed to decode words through rhyming, blending and segmenting. Teachers and parents love the lessons and activities while children find the catchy, toe-tapping tunes fun. IN ENGLISH

Songs and Activities for Early Learners™

Dynamic songs teach the alphabet, counting, parts of the body, members of the family, colors, shapes, fruit and more. Helps students of all ages to learn basic vocabulary easily. The kit includes a lyrics book with activities which teachers may reproduce for their classes. IN ENGLISH, FRENCH OR SPANISH

Thematic Songs for Learning Language™

Delightful collection of songs and activities teaching salutations, rooms of the house, pets, meals, food, silverware, transportation, communication, parts of the body, clothing, weather and prepositions. Great for ESL classes. The kit includes a lyrics book with activities teachers may reproduce for their classes. IN ENGLISH, FRENCH OR SPANISH

Reading Readiness Songs™

This great introduction to reading uses both phonics and whole language approaches. Topics covered include the alphabet, vowels, consonants, telling time, days of the week, seasons, the environment and more! The lyrics book includes helpful hints for parents and teachers. IN ENGLISH, FRENCH OR SPANISH

Grammar Grooves vol.1™

Ten songs that teach about nouns, pronouns, adjectives, verbs, tenses, adverbs and punctuation. Activities and puzzles, which may be reproduced, are included in the lyrics book to help reinforce learning even further. A complement of music tracks to the 10 songs is included for karaoke performances. Also great for music night productions. IN ENGLISH, FRENCH OR SPANISH

Lullabies Around the World - MULTICULTURAL

*** Parents' Choice Award Winner! ***

Traditional lullabies sung by native singers with translated verses in English. Multicultural activities are included in the lyrics book. Includes a complement of music tracks for class performances. Pre-K - Grade 3   11 DIFFERENT LANGUAGES

Celebrate the Human Race

Award-winning songs based on the lives and cultures of children whose homelands boast the Seven Natural Wonders of the World. This is an incredible resource. Each song is musically representative of the culture. Paper dolls and costumes are included in the reproducible lyrics book. Grade: K – 3
IN ENGLISH

Healthy Habits™

*** Directors' Choice Award Winner! ***

Songs and activities for Pre-K to Grade 3 covering nutrition, the food pyramid, anatomy, dental hygiene, personal and fire safety. The lyrics book which accompanies the recording has activities which can be reproduced by the classroom teacher. A complement of music accompaniment tracks works well for performances. IN ENGLISH

The Math Unplugged™ Series

Available for Addition, Subtraction, Division and Multiplication. Tuneful songs teach kids the basic math facts. Repetitive, musical and fun. A great resource. Each audio kit includes a lyrics book with worksheet pages which may be reproduced.
IN ENGLISH

Check out these great resource books full of reproducible activities and exercises for the classroom.

Bilingual Kids™ Volumes 1-4

Reproducible black-line thematic lessons and exercises, based on the *Bilingual Songs* series, teach the basic alphabet, counting to 100, days of the week, months of the year, greetings, colors, food, animals, parts of the body, clothing, family members, emotions, places in the community and the countryside, measurement, opposites, gender, articles, plural forms of nouns, adjectives, pronouns, adverbs of frequency, question words and much more!
ENGLISH-SPANISH and ENGLISH-FRENCH

Spanish for Kids: Beginning Lessons

Reproducible, black-line thematic lessons and exercises in Spanish, based on *Español para principiantes*, teach the alphabet, numbers, days of the week, opposites, colors, family members, body parts and much more! Lessons are enhanced with information about Hispanic culture. 64 pages.
Beginner level. ALSO AVAILABLE IN FRENCH

Spanish for Kids: Thematic Lessons

Reproducible, black-line thematic lessons and exercises in Spanish, based on *Canciones temáticas*, teach common expressions, salutations, time, modes of transportation, pets, prepositions and much more! Lessons are enhanced with information about Hispanic culture. 64 pages. Beginner level.
ALSO AVAILABLE IN FRENCH

Thematic French Lessons & Activities

Seasons / Les saisons, vol. 1
Holidays / Les fêtes, vol. 2
French across the curriculum! Liven up your classes all year long with these reproducible French lessons and activities based on holidays and seasons. Includes: dictations, conjugation exercises practicing –er, –ir, –re verbs, avoir and être in the present tense, word searches, crossword puzzles, art projects and brainteasers. 64 pages. IN FRENCH

Please visit our web site, a great meeting place
for kids, teachers and parents on the Internet.

www.SongsThatTeach.com

For help finding a retailer near you contact
Sara Jordan Publishing 1-800-567-7733